Soft and easy care for baby knits, Lion Brand® Ice Cream® is a light weight self-striping yarn that blends unique and cheerful color combinations to create delightful colorways. There's even a sophisticated gender-neutral tonal grey shade. This will be your next favorite yarn for baby shower gifts or your own baby project!

About Lion Brand® Yarn Company

Lion Brand® Yarn Company is a 5th generation, family-owned and operated business, and a beloved American brand since 1878. The company is devoted to inspiring and educating knitters and crocheters with yarns, patterns, how-tos, and ideas that elevate their yarn crafting experience.

LEISURE ARTS, INC.
Maumelle, Arkansas

Log Cabin

EASY

SIZE: About 30" x 30" (76 cm x 76 cm)

SHOPPING LIST

Yarn (Light Weight) LIGHT 3

LION BRAND® ICE CREAM® (Art. #923)

- ☐ #202 Lemon Swirl - 1 ball (A)
- ☐ #203 Blueberry - 1 ball (B)
- ☐ #208 Mint - 1 ball (C)
- ☐ #211 Lemon Meringue - 1 ball (D)

Knitting Needles

LION BRAND® Straight knitting needles,

- ☐ Size 5 (3.75 mm) **or** size needed for gauge

Additional Supply

- ☐ LION BRAND® large-eyed blunt needle

GAUGE

20½ sts + 36 rows = about 4" (10 cm) in Garter st (k every row).

1 Square = about 7" x 7" (18 cm x 18 cm).

BE SURE TO CHECK YOUR GAUGE.

NOTES

1. Afghan is made from 16 Squares sewn together following a diagram.
2. Squares are worked log cabin-style, as shown in Square Layout Diagram. First a small square is worked. The "logs" are worked from stitches picked up on the small square.
3. A border is worked along each of the 4 sides of the assembled Afghan.

SQUARES

(Make 16 as follows: 4 with D for small square and A for logs; 6 with D for small square and B for logs; and 6 with D for small square and C for logs)

Small Square

With D, cast on 9 sts.

Work in Garter st (k every row) for 16 rows.

Bind off.

First Log

From RS with log color, pick up and k9 sts evenly spaced along left side edge of small square.

Work in Garter st for 15 rows.

Bind off.

Second Log

From RS with log color, pick up and k18 sts evenly spaced along bound-off edge of small square and right side edge of first log.

Work in Garter st for 15 rows.

Bind off.

Third Log

From RS with log color, pick up and k18 sts evenly spaced along left side edge of second log and bound-off edge of first log.

Work in Garter st for 15 rows.

Bind off.

Fourth Log

From RS with log color, pick up and k27 sts evenly spaced along bound-off edge of second log and right side edge of third log.

Work in Garter st for 15 rows.

Bind off.

Fifth Log

From RS with log color, pick up and k27 sts evenly spaced along left side edge of fourth log and bound-off edge of third log.

Work in Garter st for 15 rows.

Bind off.

Sixth Log

From RS with log color, pick up and k36 sts evenly spaced along bound-off edge of fourth log and right side edge of fifth log.

Work in Garter st for 15 rows.

Bind off.

SQUARE LAYOUT

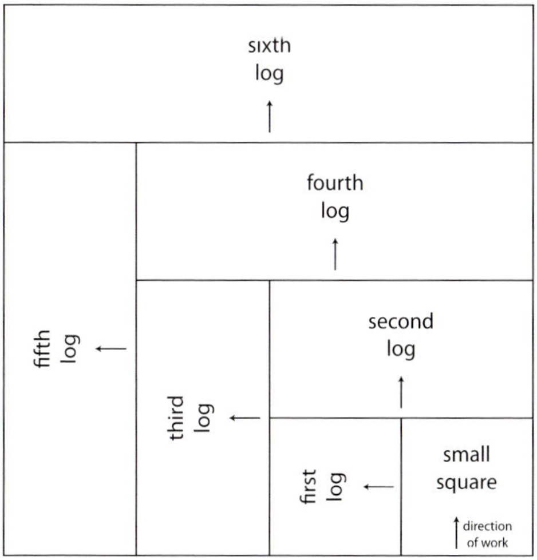

FINISHING

Following diagram, sew Squares into 4 strips of 4 Squares each. Sew strips together to make Afghan.

ASSEMBLY DIAGRAM

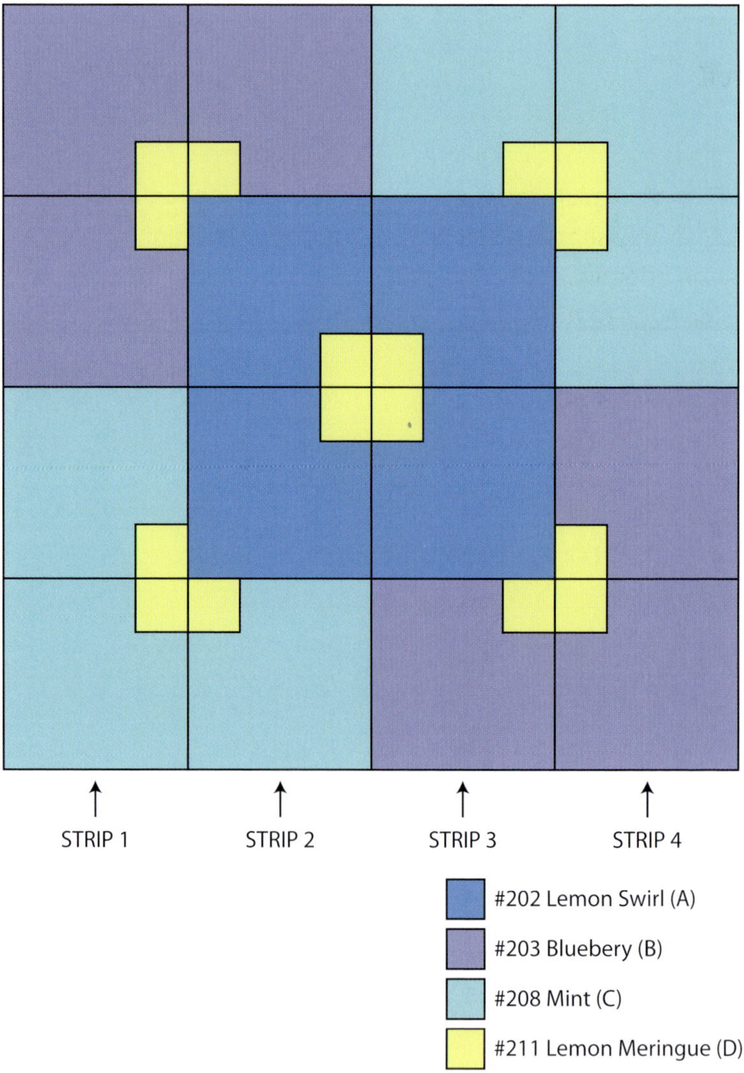

First Border

From RS with D, pick up and k144 sts evenly spaced along any side edge of Afghan.

Work in Garter st for 7 rows.

Bind off.

Second and Third Borders

From RS with D, pick up and k148 sts evenly spaced along left side edge of previous border and next side edge of Afghan.

Work in Garter st for 7 rows.

Bind off.

Repeat for third border.

Fourth Border

From RS with D, pick up and k152 sts evenly spaced along left side edge of third border, last side edge of Afghan, and right side edge of first border.

Work in Garter st for 7 rows.

Bind off.

Weave in ends.

Four Square

BEGINNER

SIZE: About 35" x 35" (89 cm x 89 cm), including borders

SHOPPING LIST

Yarn (Light Weight)

LIGHT 3

LION BRAND® ICE CREAM® (Art. #923)

☐ #212 Coffee - 2 balls (A)

☐ #208 Mint - 3 balls (B)

Knitting Needles

LION BRAND® Straight knitting needles,

☐ Size 5 (3.75 mm) **or** size needed for gauge

Additional Supply

☐ LION BRAND® large-eyed blunt needle

GAUGE

20 sts = about 4" (10 cm) in Garter st (knit every st on every row).

BE SURE TO CHECK YOUR GAUGE.

STITCH GUIDE

KNIT IN FRONT AND BACK (abbreviated kfb)

Knit next st without removing it from left hand needle, then k through back of same st – 1 st increased.

MAKE 1 (abbreviated M1)

An increase worked by lifting the horizontal strand lying between needles and placing it onto the left needle. Knit this new stitch through the back loop – 1 st increased.

NOTES

1. 4 Squares are worked separately, then sewn together to make the Afghan.
2. Squares are worked in Garter st (knit every st on every row) from corner to corner, working increases on the first half and decreases on the second.
3. Borders are worked with increases to create a miter at each corner.

SQUARES (make 4)

With A, cast on 3 sts.

Increase Half

Row 1 (RS): K1, M1, k1, M1, k1 – you will have 5 sts.

Row 2: Knit.

Row 3 (Increase Row): K1, kfb, k to last 2 sts, kfb, k1 – 7 sts.

Rows 4-57: Rep Rows 2 and 3 – 61 sts at the end of Row 57.

Row 58: Knit.

Change to B.

Row 59: With B, rep Row 3 – 63 sts.

Rows 60-117: With B, rep Rows 2 and 3 – 121 sts at the end of Row 117.

Decrease Half

Row 118: Knit.

Row 119 (Decrease Row): K1, k2tog, k to last 3 sts, k2tog, k1 – you will have 119 sts.

Rows 120-233: Rep Rows 118 and 119 – 5 sts at the end of Row 233.

Row 234: Knit.

Row 235: K1, k3tog, k1 – 3 sts.

Bind off.

FINISHING

With cast on corners of each Square at center, sew Squares together.

Borders

From RS with A and working along one side of Afghan, pick up and k155 sts evenly spaced along edge.

Row 1 (WS): Knit.

Row 2: K 1, kfb, k to last 2 sts, kfb, k1 – 157 sts.

Repeat Rows 1 and 2 for 9 more times – 175 sts.

Next Row: Knit.

Bind off.

Repeat border along each of the 3 remaining sides of the Afghan. Sew shaped ends of borders together at each corner of Afghan.

Weave in ends.

Triangles Squared

EASY

SIZE: About 30" x 30" (76 cm x 76 cm)

SHOPPING LIST

Yarn (Light Weight) LIGHT 3

LION BRAND® ICE CREAM® (Art. #923)

- ☐ #206 Tutti Frutti - 1 ball (A)
- ☐ #203 Blueberry - 1 ball (B)
- ☐ #204 Banana Split - 1 ball (C)
- ☐ #201 Cotton Candy - 1 ball (D)

Knitting Needles

LION BRAND® Straight knitting needles,

- ☐ Size 5 (3.75 mm) **or** size needed for gauge

Additional Supply

- ☐ LION BRAND® large-eyed blunt needle

GAUGE

20 sts + 40 rows = about 4" (10 cm) in Garter st (knit every st on every row).
BE SURE TO CHECK YOUR GAUGE.

STITCH GUIDE

KNIT IN FRONT AND BACK (abbreviated kfb)

Knit next st without removing it from left hand needle, then k through back of same st – 1 st increased.

NOTES

1. A Center Square is worked first, then stitches are picked up along the sides of the square to make the Afghan.
2. Stitches for the borders are picked up along each edge of the completed Afghan. The border is shaped with mitered and seamed corners.

AFGHAN

Center Square

With A, loosely cast on 40 sts.

Work in Garter st (knit every st on every row) for 80 rows. The last row is a WS row.

First Triangle

Next Row (RS): With B, knit.

Decrease row (WS): With B, knit to last 2 sts, k2tog.

Repeat last row until only 2 sts remain.

K2tog, then cut yarn and fasten off last st.

Second Triangle

From RS with B, pick up and k40 sts evenly spaced across one side edge of center square.

Decrease row (WS): With B, knit to last 2 sts, k2tog.

Repeat last row until only 2 sts remain.

K2tog, then cut yarn and fasten off last st.

Third and Fourth Triangles

Working along next side edge of Center Square, work as for second triangle.

Note that when the fourth triangle has been completed, you'll have created a square; this is the larger center square.

Fifth Triangle

From RS with C, pick up and k55 sts evenly spaced across one side edge of the larger center square.

Decrease row (WS): With C, knit to last 2 sts, k2tog.

Repeat last row until only 2 sts remain.

K2tog, then cut yarn and fasten off last st.

Sixth-Eighth Triangles

Working along next side edge of larger center square, work as for fifth triangle.

Note that when the eighth triangle has been completed, you'll have created a square; this is the largest center square.

Ninth Triangle

From RS with C, pick up and k80 sts evenly spaced across one side edge of the largest center square.

Decrease row (WS): With B, knit to last 2 sts, k2tog.

Repeat last row until only 2 sts remain.

K2tog, then cut yarn and fasten off last st.

Tenth-Twelfth Triangles

Working along next side edge of largest center square, work as for ninth triangle.

FINISHING

Border

From RS with A, pick up and k110 sts evenly spaced across one edge of Afghan.

Row 1: Kfb, knit to last st, kfb in last st - at the end of this row, you'll have 112 sts.

Row 2: Knit.

Rep Rows 1 and 2, changing color as follows:
Work 13 more rows with A, then work 16 rows with B and 7 rows with C – you'll have 148 sts.

Bind off.

Rep border along each of the 3 remaining sides of Afghan. Sew ends of borders together.

Weave in ends.

Hexagon

EASY

SIZE: About 40" (101.5 cm) from point to point

SHOPPING LIST

Yarn (Light Weight) LIGHT 3

LION BRAND® ICE CREAM® (Art. #923)

- ☐ #200 Cookies and Cream - 2 balls (A)
- ☐ #211 Lemon Meringue - 2 balls (B)

Knitting Needles

Circular, 36" (91.5 cm) long,

- ☐ Size 5 (3.75 mm) **or** size needed for gauge

Additional Supplies

- ☐ LION BRAND® stitch markers
- ☐ LION BRAND® large-eyed blunt needle

GAUGE

20 sts = about 4" (10 cm) in Garter st
(knit every st on every row)
BE SURE TO CHECK YOUR GAUGE

NOTES

1. Afghan is worked in 6 triangle sections.
2. A circular needle is used to accommodate the large number of sts. Work back and forth in rows on the circular needle, just as if working on straight needles.

AFGHAN

First Triangle

With A, cast on 100 sts.

Rows 1-3: Knit.

Row 4 (Decrease Row): K1, k2tog, k to last 3 sts, k2tog, k1 – you will have 98 sts.

Rows 5-192: Rep Rows 1-4. At the end of Row 192, you will have 4 sts remaining.

Rows 193-195: Knit.

Row 196: K2tog twice – 2 sts.

Row 197: Knit.

Row 198: K2tog.

Fasten off.

Second Triangle

Note: Either side of the first triangle can be the right side. Simply decide which side you'd like to be the right side, then place a marker on it.

From right side, with B and working along left edge of first triangle, pick up and knit 100 sts evenly spaced along edge, then work second triangle same as first.

Third, Fourth, Fifth and Sixth Triangles

Work same as second triangle, picking up sts along edge of previous triangle, using A for third and fifth triangles and B for the fourth and sixth.

FINISHING

Sew edges of sixth and first triangles together.

Weave in ends.

Mitered Squares

EASY +

SIZE: About 32 x 32 in. (81.5 x 81.5 cm)

SHOPPING LIST

Yarn (Light Weight) LIGHT 3

LION BRAND® ICE CREAM® (Art. #923)

- ☐ #206 Tutti Frutti - 2 balls (A)
- ☐ #207 Strawberry - 1 ball (B)
- ☐ #211 Lemon Meringue - 1 ball (C)
- ☐ #208 Mint - 1 ball (D)

Knitting Needles

LION BRAND® Straight knitting needles,

- ☐ Size 6 (4 mm) **or** size needed for gauge

Circular, 60" (152.5 cm) long,

- ☐ Size 6 (4 mm)

Additional Supplies

- ☐ LION BRAND® stitch markers
- ☐ LION BRAND® large-eyed blunt needle

GAUGE

Square 1 = about 8" x 8" (20.5 cm x 20.5 cm).
BE SURE TO CHECK YOUR GAUGE.

STITCH GUIDE

SLIP, SLIP, KNIT (abbreviated ssk)

Slip next 2 sts as if to knit, one at a time, to right-hand needle; insert left-hand needle into fronts of these 2 sts and knit them together – 1 st decreased.

NOTES

1. Square 1 is worked first, then subsequent squares are worked from stitches picked up from previous squares.
2. The miter on each square is shaped by working decreases.
3. A long circular needle is used for the edging.

SQUARE 1

With straight needles and A, cast on 70 sts.

Row 1 (WS): K35, place marker (pm), k35.

Row 2 (Decrease Row): Knit to 2 sts before marker, k2tog, slip marker, ssk, knit to end of row – at the end of this row you will have 68 sts.

Row 3: Knit.

Rows 4-13: Rep Rows 2 and 3 – 58 sts at the end of Row 12.
Change to B.

Rows 14-27: With B, rep Rows 2 and 3 – 44 sts at the end of Row 26.
Change to C.

Rows 28-41: With C, rep Rows 2 and 3 – 30 sts at the end of Row 40.
Change to D.

Rows 42-55: With D, rep Rows 2 and 3 – 16 sts at the end of Row 54.
Change to A.

Rows 56-67: With A, rep Rows 2 and 3 – 4 sts at the end of Row 66.

Row 68: With A, k2tog, ssk – 2 sts.

Row 69: K2tog.

Fasten off last st.

Note: Before beginning Squares 2-16, refer to diagram for where to pick up stitches.

SQUARE 2

With A, cast on 35 sts, pm, from RS and following diagram, pick up and k35 sts evenly spaced across edge of Square 1 – 70 sts.

Repeat Rows 1-69 of Square 1.

SQUARE 3

With A, cast on 35 sts, pm, from RS and following diagram, pick up and k35 sts evenly spaced across edge of Square 2 – 70 sts.

Repeat Rows 1-69 of Square 1.

SQUARE 4

With A, cast on 35 sts, pm, from RS and following diagram, pick up and k35 sts evenly spaced across edge of Square 3 – 70 sts.

Repeat Rows 1-69 of Square 1.

SQUARE 5

From RS with A and following diagram, pick up and k35 sts evenly spaced across top of Square 1, pm, cast on 35 sts – 70 sts.

Repeat Rows 1-69 of Square 1.

SQUARE 6

From RS with A and following diagram, pick up and k35 sts evenly spaced across top of Square 2, pm, then pick up and k35 sts evenly spaced along side of Square 5 – 70 sts.

Repeat Rows 1-69 of Square 1.

SQUARE 7

From RS with A and following diagram, pick up and k35 sts evenly spaced across top of Square 3, pm, then pick up and k35 sts evenly spaced along side of Square 6 – 70 sts.

Repeat Rows 1-69 of Square 1.

SQUARE 8

From RS with A and following diagram, pick up and k35 sts evenly spaced across top of Square 4, pm, then pick up and k35 sts evenly spaced along side of Square 7 – 70 sts.

Repeat Rows 1-69 of Square 1.

SQUARE 9

From RS with A and following diagram, pick up and k35 sts evenly spaced across top of Square 5, pm, cast on 35 sts – 70 sts.

Repeat Rows 1-69 of Square 1.

SQUARE 10

From RS with A and following diagram, pick up and k35 sts evenly spaced across top of Square 6, pm, then pick up and k35 sts evenly spaced along side of Square 9 – 70 sts.

Repeat Rows 1-69 of Square 1.

SQUARE 11

From RS with A and following diagram, pick up and k35 sts evenly spaced across top of Square 7, pm, then pick up and k35 sts evenly spaced along side of Square 10 – 70 sts.

Repeat Rows 1-69 of Square 1.

SQUARE 12

From RS with A and following diagram, pick up and k35 sts evenly spaced across top of Square 8, pm, then pick up and k35 sts evenly spaced along side of Square 11 – 70 sts.

Repeat Rows 1-69 of Square 1.

SQUARE 13

From RS with A and following diagram, pick up and k35 sts evenly spaced across top of Square 9, pm, cast on 35 sts – 70 sts.

Repeat Rows 1-69 of Square 1.

SQUARE 14

From RS with A and following diagram, pick up and k35 sts evenly spaced across top of Square 10, pm, then pick up and k35 sts evenly spaced along side of Square 13 – 70 sts.

Repeat Rows 1-69 of Square 1.

SQUARE 15

From RS with A and following diagram, pick up and k35 sts evenly spaced across top of Square 11, pm, then pick up and k35 sts evenly spaced along side of Square 14 – 70 sts.

Repeat Rows 1-69 of Square 1.

SQUARE 16

From RS with A and following diagram, pick up and k35 sts evenly spaced across top of Square 12, pm, then pick up and k35 sts evenly spaced along side of Square 15 – 70 sts.
Repeat Rows 1-69 of Square 1.

FINISHING
Edging

From RS with circular needle and A, beginning anywhere along outside edge of Afghan, pick up and k140 sts evenly spaced across each side of Afghan – 560 sts.
Place marker and join for working in the round by purling the first st on the left-hand needle with the working yarn from the right-hand needle.

Purl one rnd.

Bind off.

Weave in ends.

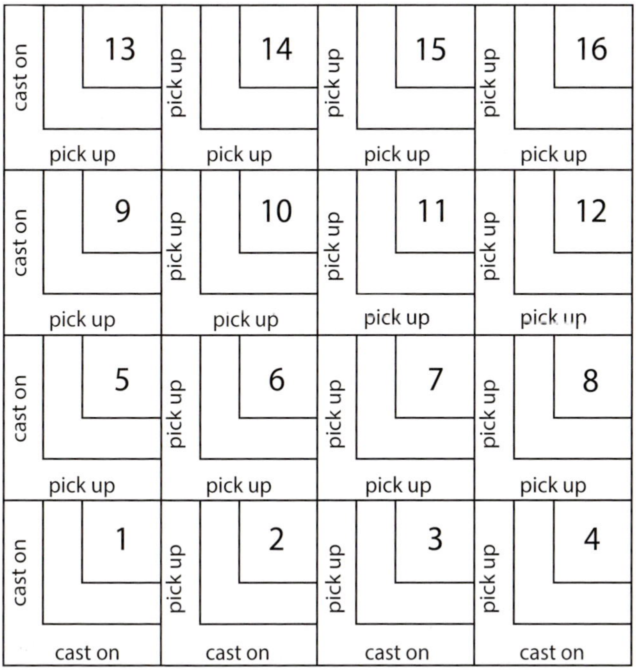

Right Angles

EASY

SIZE: About 30" x 30" (76 cm x 76 cm)

SHOPPING LIST

Yarn (Light Weight) LIGHT 3

LION BRAND® ICE CREAM® (Art. #923)

- ☐ #203 Blueberry - 1 ball (A)
- ☐ #201 Cotton Candy - 1 ball (B)
- ☐ #211 Lemon Meringue - 1 ball (C)

Knitting Needles

Circular, 36" (91.5 cm) long,

- ☐ Size 5 (3.75 mm) **or** size needed for gauge

Additional Supply

- ☐ LION BRAND® large-eyed blunt needle

GAUGE

20 sts = about 4" (10 cm) in Garter st
(knit every st on every row).
BE SURE TO CHECK YOUR GAUGE.

NOTES

1. The Afghan is worked in one piece in 2 sections.
2. Stitches for the second section are picked up from the first section.
3. A circular needle is used to accommodate the large number of sts. Work back and forth in rows on the circular needle, just as if working on straight needles.
4. To make it easier to count your rows, mark the first row as a right side row. For every 2 rows you knit, one Garter "ridge" will be completed. At the end of 100 rows, you should have 50 ridges and the last row you work will be on the wrong side.

AFGHAN

First Section

With A, cast on 75 sts.

Work in Garter st (knit every st on every row) for 100 rows.

Change to B and continue in Garter st for 100 rows, then change to C and continue in Garter st for 100 rows.

Bind off.

Second Section

From RS with B, pick up and k150 sts evenly spaced across right side edge of Afghan.

Work in Garter st for 49 rows.

Change to A and work in Garter st for 50 rows.

Change to C and work in Garter st for 50 rows.

Bind off.

FINISHING

Weave in ends.

Simple Diagonal

BEGINNER

SIZE: About 32" x 32" (81.5 cm x 81.5 cm)

SHOPPING LIST

Yarn (Light Weight) 3

LION BRAND® ICE CREAM® (Art. #923)

☐ #206 Tutti Frutti - 2 balls (A)

☐ #201 Cotton Candy - 2 balls (B)

Knitting Needles

LION BRAND® Circular knitting needle, 29" (73.5 cm) long,

☐ Size 10.5 (6.5 mm) **or** size needed for gauge

Additional Supply

☐ LION BRAND® large-eyed blunt needle

GAUGE

13 sts = about 4" (10 cm) in Garter st (knit every stitch on every row) with one strand each of A and B held together. BE SURE TO CHECK YOUR GAUGE.

STITCH GUIDE

YARN OVER (abbreviated Yo)

An increase that also creates a small decorative hole (eyelet) in the fabric, worked as follows:

1. Bring yarn to front, between the needles.
2. Take yarn to back, over the right hand needle. This creates the new st. You are now ready to proceed with the next st as instructed.

NOTES

1. Afghan is worked in Garter st (knit every stitch on every row) from corner to corner with 2 strands of yarn held together. The first half of the Afghan is shaped with yarn over increases and the second half is shaped with decreases.
2. A circular needle is used to accommodate the large number of stitches. Work back and forth in rows on the circular needle as if knitting with straight needles.

AFGHAN

With one strand each of A and B held together, cast on 5 sts.

Increase Half

Row 1: Knit.

Row 2: K3, yo, k2 – 6 sts.

Row 3: K3, yo, k3 – 7 sts.

Row 4: K3, yo, k to end of row.

Repeat Row 4 until you have 140 sts.

Decrease Half

Next Row (Decrease Row): K2, k2tog, yo, k2tog, k to end of row.

Repeat last row until 5 sts remain.

Bind off.

FINISHING

Weave in ends.

Round Ruffled

EASY

SIZE Finished Diameter: About 32" (81.5 cm)

SHOPPING LIST

Yarn (Light Weight) LIGHT 3

LION BRAND® ICE CREAM® (Art. #923)

- ☐ #204 Banana Split - 1 ball (A)
- ☐ #208 Mint - 1 ball (B)
- ☐ #206 Tutti Frutti - 1 ball (C)
- ☐ #207 Strawberry - 1 ball (D)

Knitting Needles

LION BRAND® double-pointed knitting needles,

- ☐ Size 5 (3.75 mm) **or** size needed for gauge

Circulars, 24" (61 cm) and 40" (101.5 cm) long,

- ☐ Size 5 (3.75 mm) **or** size needed for gauge

Additional Supplies

- ☐ LION BRAND® stitch markers
- ☐ LION BRAND® large-eyed blunt needle

GAUGE

72 sts in the round = about 7½" (19 cm) in diameter.
BE SURE TO CHECK YOUR GAUGE.

STITCH GUIDE

KNIT IN FRONT AND BACK (abbreviated kfb)

Knit next st without removing it from left-hand needle, then k through back of same st – 1 st increased.

PURL INTO BACK AND FRONT (abbreviated pfb)

Purl through back of next st without removing it from the left-hand needle, then purl through front of same st – 1 st increased.

NOTES

1. The Afghan is worked in one piece in the round.
2. Work begins on double-pointed needles, then changes to a circular needle when stitches have been sufficiently increased.

AFGHAN

With double-pointed needles and A, cast on 9 sts.

Divide sts onto 3 double-pointed needles, with 3 sts on each needle. Place marker (pm) for beg of rnd and join by working the first st on the left-hand needle with the working yarn from the right-hand needle, and being careful not to twist sts.
As you work, slip the marker on each round as you come to it.

Rnd 1: Knit.

Rnd 2: Kfb in each st around – you will have 18 sts.

Rnds 3-5: Knit.

Notes

1. The increase rnds on the remainder of the Afghan are purled. This makes a decorative ridge on the Afghan.
2. Follow the instructions below AND AT THE SAME TIME, change yarn color as follows:
   With A, work until piece measures about 3" (7.5 cm) from center.
   Change to B and work until piece measures about 8" (20.5 cm) from center.
   Change to C and work until piece measures about 12" (30.5 cm) from center.
   Change to D and work until piece measures about 16" (40.5 cm) from center.

Increase Rnd: Pfb in each st around – 36 sts.

Knit 6 rnds.

Repeat Increase Rnd – you will have 72 sts.

Knit 12 rnds.

Repeat Increase Rnd, changing from double-pointed needles to the shorter circular needle as you work – 144 sts.

Knit 24 rnds.

Repeat Increase Rnd, changing to the longer circular needle as you work – 288 sts.

Knit 48 rnds.

Repeat Increase Rnd – 576 sts.

Knit for about 3" (7.5 cm).

Border

Continue with D and work in Garter st worked in the rnd (knit one rnd, purl one rnd) for about 1" (2.5 cm).

Bind off as follows: Knit 2 sts, *insert point of left hand needle into front of 2 sts on right hand needle and knit 2 together through back loop, knit next st, repeat from * until all sts have been bound off.

Fasten off last st.

FINISHING

Weave in ends.

Happy Valley

EASY

SIZE: About 29 x 29 in. (73.5 x 73.5 cm)

SHOPPING LIST

Yarn (Light Weight 3)

LION BRAND® ICE CREAM® (Art. #923)

- ☐ #209 Birthday Cake - 1 ball (A)
- ☐ #211 Lemon Meringue - 1 ball (B)
- ☐ #208 Mint - 1 ball (C)

Knitting Needles

LION BRAND® knitting needles,

- ☐ Size 5 (3.75 mm) **or** size needed for gauge

Additional Supplies

- ☐ LION BRAND® stitch markers
- ☐ LION BRAND® large-eyed blunt needle

GAUGE

20 sts + 40 rows = about 4" (10 cm) in Garter st (k every row).

1 Diamond = about 2½" x 2½" (6.5 cm x 6.5 cm).

BE SURE TO CHECK YOUR GAUGE.

STITCH GUIDE

SLIP, SLIP, KNIT (abbreviated ssk)

Slip next 2 sts as if to knit, one at a time, to right-hand needle; insert left-hand needle into fronts of these 2 sts and knit them together – 1 st decreased.

NOTES

1. Afghan is worked in one piece beginning with 9 mitered Diamonds.
2. Diamonds are mitered by working a double decrease (k3tog) at the center of every RS row.
3. Diamonds are worked in rows, from right to left.
4. To slip the first stitch of each row, you can slip as if to knit or slip as if to purl, whichever looks best with your knitting style.

STRIPE SEQUENCE

Work *1 row of Diamonds with A, 1 row of Diamonds with B, and 1 row of Diamonds with C; rep from * for Stripe Sequence.

FIRST ROW DIAMONDS (make 9)

Note: For this row, you'll make 9 separate Diamonds, then join them together when working the Second Row of Diamonds.

With A, cast on 21 sts.

Row 1 (WS): Knit.

Row 2: K9, k3tog, place a marker on st just made, k9 – you will have 19 sts in this row.
Note: Place marker on st, not on needle so that marker does not become entangled in later rows.

Row 3: Knit.

Row 4: K to 1 st before marked st, k3tog, move marker to st just made, k to end of row – 17 sts.

Rows 5-18: Rep Rows 3 and 4 seven times – 3 sts rem at the end of Row 18.

Row 19 (WS): K3tog – 1 st. Fasten off. Rep until you have 9 Diamonds.

SECOND ROW OF DIAMONDS

Notes

1. You'll be picking up sts along the top edges of the 9 First Row Diamonds to join them and to begin the Diamonds of this Second Row.
2. When picking up sts, work from the RS and hold the Diamonds with the last row (Row 19) on top.

First Half Diamond

From RS with B, pick up and k11 sts evenly spaced along upper right edge of one First Row Diamond.

Row 1 (WS): Knit.

Row 2: Sl 1, k2tog, k to end of row – 10 sts.

Rows 3-16: Rep Rows 1 and 2 seven times – 3 sts rem at the end of Row 16.

Row 17: Knit.

Row 18: Sl 1, k2tog – 2 sts.

Row 19 (WS): K2tog – 1 st. Fasten off.

Next 8 Full Diamonds

From RS with B, pick up and k10 sts evenly spaced along upper left edge of same First Row Diamond, cast on 1 st, pick up and k10 sts evenly spaced along upper right edge of another separate First Row Diamond – 21 sts.

Rows 1-19: Work same as Rows 1-19 of First Row Diamonds. Fasten off.

Rep until 8 Full Diamonds have been made and all First Row Diamonds have been joined tog.

Last Half Diamond

From RS with B, pick up and k11 sts evenly spaced along upper left edge of same (last) First Row Diamond.

Row 1 (WS): Sl 1, k to end of row.

Row 2: K to last 3 sts, ssk, k1 – 10 sts.

Rows 3-16: Rep Rows 1 and 2 seven times – 3 sts rem at the end of Row 16.

Row 17: Sl 1, k to end of row.

Row 18: Ssk, k1 – 2 sts.

Row 19 (WS): Ssk – 1 st.
Fasten off.

THIRD ROW OF DIAMONDS

Note: This row is worked from right to left along the top edge of the previous row of Diamonds.

First Full Diamond

From RS with C, pick up and k10 sts evenly spaced along upper left edge of First Half Diamond of previous row, cast on 1 st, pick up and k10 sts evenly spaced along right side edge of next Diamond – 21 sts.

Rows 1-19: Work same as Rows 1-19 of First Row Diamonds.
Fasten off.

Next 7 Full Diamonds

From RS with C, pick up and k10 sts evenly spaced along upper left edge of same Diamond in previous row, cast on 1 st, pick up and k10 sts evenly spaced along upper right edge of next Diamond in previous row – 21 sts.

Rows 1-19: Work same as Rows 1-19 of First Row Diamonds. Fasten off.

Rep until a total of 8 Full Diamonds have been made in this Row.

Last Full Diamond

From RS with C, pick up and k10 sts evenly spaced along upper left edge of same (last) Full Diamond in previous row, cast on 1 st, pick up and k10 sts evenly spaced along upper right edge of Last Half Diamond in previous row – 21 sts.

Rows 1-19: Work same as Rows 1-19 of First Row Diamonds. Fasten off.

FOURTH ROW OF DIAMONDS

Note: You will be working from right to left along the top edge of the previous row of Diamonds.

First Half Diamond

From RS with A, pick up and k11 sts evenly spaced along upper right edge of first Diamond in previous row of Diamonds.

Rows 1-19: Work same as Rows 1-19 of First Half Diamond of Second Row of Diamonds. Fasten off.

Next 8 Full Diamonds

From RS with A, pick up and k10 sts evenly spaced along upper left edge of same Diamond in previous row, cast on 1 st, pick up and k10 sts evenly spaced along upper right edge of next Diamond in previous row – 21 sts.

Rows 1-19: Work same as Rows 1-19 of First Row Diamonds. Fasten off.

Rep until 8 Full Diamonds have been made in this row.

Last Half Diamond

From RS with A, pick up and k11 sts evenly spaced along upper left edge of same (last) Diamond in previous row.

Rows 1-19: Work same as Rows 1-19 of Last Half Diamond of Second Row of Diamonds. Fasten off.

NEXT 17 ROWS OF DIAMONDS

Rep Third and Fourth Rows of Diamonds and continue to change color as in Stripe Sequence until a total of 21 Rows of Diamonds have been worked, end with a Third Row of Diamonds as the last Row of Diamonds you work.

FINISHING

Weave in ends.

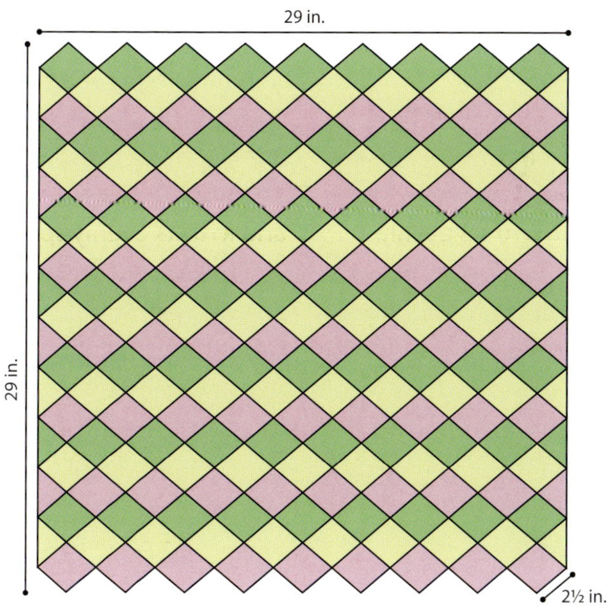

General Instructions

ABBREVIATIONS

beg = begin(ning)(s)
kfb = knit in the front and back
k = knit
k2tog = knit 2 stitches together
pfb = purl in the front and back
rep = repeat
rem = remain(ing)(s)
RS = right side
rnd(s) = round(s)
st(s) = stitch(es)
tog = together
WS = wrong side

* — When you see an asterisk used within a pattern row, the symbol indicates that later you will be told to repeat a portion of the instruction. Most often the instructions will say, repeat from * so many times.

( ) or **[ ]** — Sets off a short number of stitches that are repeated or indicates additional information.

– When you see – (dash) followed by a number of stitches, this tells you how many stitches you will have at the end of a row or round.

GAUGE

Never underestimate the importance of gauge. Achieving the correct gauge assures that the finished size of your piece matches the finished size given in the pattern.

CHECKING YOUR GAUGE

Work a swatch that is at least 4" (10 cm) square. Use the suggested needle size and the number of stitches given. If your swatch is larger than 4" (10 cm), you need to work it again using smaller needles; if it is smaller than 4" (10 cm), try it with larger needles. This might require a swatch or two to get the exact gauge given in the pattern.

METRICS

As a handy reference, keep in mind that 1 ounce = approximately 28 grams and 1" = 2.5 centimeters.

TERMS

fasten off — To end your piece, you need to simply cut and pull the yarn through the last loop left on the needle. This keeps the last stitch intact and prevents the work from unraveling.

right side — Refers to the front of the piece.

LION BRAND® ICE CREAM®
Article #923

Weight Category: 3 - Light Weight: Baby items
Solids: 3.5oz/100g (394yd/360m)

Gauge:
Knit: 22 sts x 30 rows = 4 inches on size 5 [3.75 mm] needles
Crochet: 16 sc x 20 rows = 4 inches on H-8 [5 mm] hook

Fiber Content: 100% Acrylic

Product Care Instructions: Machine wash and dry.

VISIT LionBrand.com FOR:
- Learn to Knit & Crochet Instructions
- Weekly newsletter with articles, tips, and updates
- Store Locator

We have made every effort to ensure that these instructions are accurate and complete. We cannot, however, be responsible for human error, typographical mistakes, or variations in individual work.

Copyright © 2018 by Leisure Arts, Inc., 104 Champs Blvd., STE 100, Maumelle, AR 72113-6738, www.leisurearts.com. All rights reserved. This publication is protected under federal copyright laws. Reproduction or distribution of this publication or any other Leisure Arts publication, including publications which are out of print, is prohibited unless specifically authorized. This includes, but is not limited to, any form of reproduction or distribution on or through the Internet, including posting, scanning, or e-mail transmission.

©2018 Lion Brand Yarn Company, all rights reserved.